THE GREATEST PLAYERS

BASEBALL

Steve Goldsworthy and Aaron Carr

AV² provides enriched content that supplements and complements this book. Weigl's AV² books strive to create inspired learning and engage young minds in a total learning experience.

Your AV² Media Enhanced books come alive with...

Audio
Listen to sections of the book read aloud.

Key Words
Study vocabulary, and complete a matching word activity.

Video
Watch informative video clips.

Quizzes
Test your knowledge.

Embedded Weblinks
Gain additional information for research.

Slide Show
View images and captions, and prepare a presentation.

Try This!
Complete activities and hands-on experiments.

... and much, much more!

Go to **www.av2books.com**, and enter this book's unique code.

BOOK CODE

N 8 4 8 2 6 9

AV² by Weigl brings you media enhanced books that support active learning.

Published by AV² by Weigl
350 5th Avenue, 59th Floor
New York, NY 10118
Website: www.av2books.com   www.weigl.com

Library of Congress Cataloging-in-Publication Data

Goldsworthy, Steve.
Baseball / Steve Goldsworthy and Aaron Carr.
   p. cm. -- (The greatest)
Includes bibliographical references and index.
ISBN 978-1-61690-697-9 (hardcover : alk. paper) -- ISBN 978-1-61690-702-0 (softcover : alk. paper)
1. Baseball players--United States--Biography--Juvenile literature. I. Carr, Aaron. II. Title.
GV865.A1G63 2012
796.357092'2--dc22
[B]
                              2011002299

Printed in the United States of America in North Mankato, Minnesota
1 2 3 4 5 6 7 8 9 0 15 14 13 12 11

062011
WEP290411

Project Coordinator Aaron Carr
Art Director Terry Paulhus

Photo Credits
Every reasonable effort has been made to trace ownership and to obtain permission to reprint copyright material. The publishers would be pleased to have any errors or omissions brought to their attention so that they may be corrected in subsequent printings.

Weigl acknowledges Getty Images as its primary image supplier for this title.

Contents

What is Baseball?

Introduction

The world of professional sports has a long history of great moments. The most memorable moments often come when the sport's greatest players overcome their most challenging obstacles. For the fans, these moments come to define their favorite sport. For the players, they stand as measuring posts of success.

As the oldest major professional sport in the North America, baseball has a long history that is filled with great players and great moments. These moments include Willie Mays making "The Catch" in the 1954 World Series and Hank Aaron's record-breaking 715th career **home run**. Baseball has no shortage of these moments, when the sport's brightest stars accomplished feats that ensured they would be remembered as the greatest players.

Training Camp

Baseball is played with two teams of at least nine players. One team plays defense, while the other plays offense. The defensive team spreads its players out around the field. Outfielders are positioned at left, right, and center field. Infielders cover each of the three **bases**. The shortstop and second baseman work together to cover the gaps between the bases. These players try to prevent the other team from scoring a run. The pitcher throws the ball to the catcher. These two players work together to keep players on the other team from getting a **base hit**.

Each player on the offensive team takes a turn trying to hit the ball to drive in **runs**. The team that scores the most runs through nine **innings** wins.

Hank Aaron was one of the greatest hitters of all time.

The Field

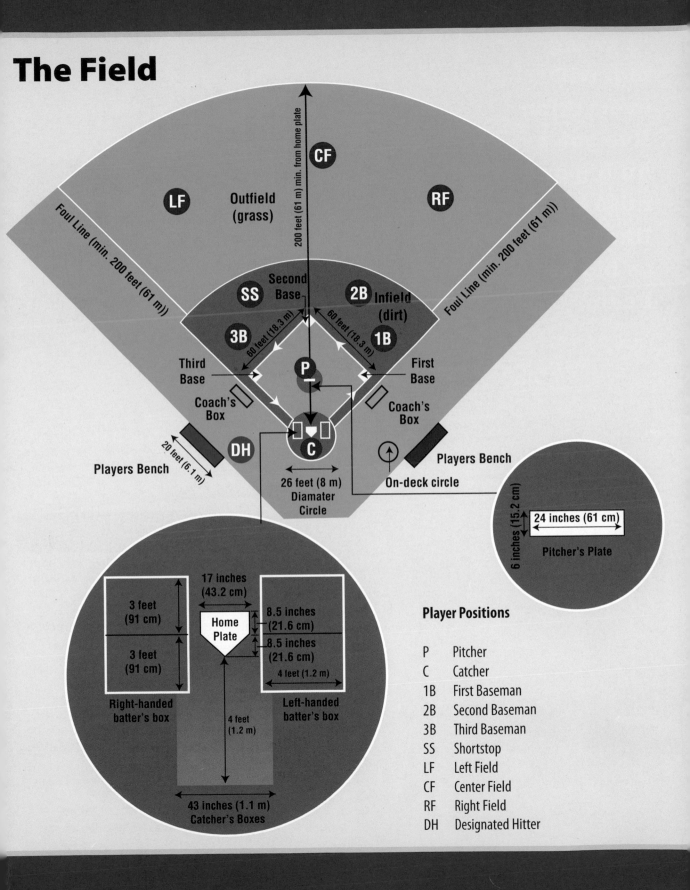

200 feet (61 m) min. from home plate

CF

LF

Outfield (grass)

RF

Foul Line (min. 200 feet (61 m))

Foul Line (min. 200 feet (61 m))

SS

Second Base

2B

Infield (dirt)

3B

60 feet (18.3 m)

60 feet (18.3 m)

1B

P

Third Base

First Base

Coach's Box

Coach's Box

20 feet (6.1 m)

DH

C

Players Bench

On-deck circle

Players Bench

26 feet (8 m) Diamater Circle

6 inches (15.2 cm)

24 inches (61 cm)

Pitcher's Plate

17 inches (43.2 cm)

3 feet (91 cm)

8.5 inches (21.6 cm)

Home Plate

8.5 inches (21.6 cm)

3 feet (91 cm)

4 feet (1.2 m)

Right-handed batter's box

Left-handed batter's box

4 feet (1.2 m)

43 inches (1.1 m) Catcher's Boxes

Player Positions

P	Pitcher
C	Catcher
1B	First Baseman
2B	Second Baseman
3B	Third Baseman
SS	Shortstop
LF	Left Field
CF	Center Field
RF	Right Field
DH	Designated Hitter

> "I swing big, with everything I've got. I hit big or I miss big. I like to live as big as I can."

Babe Ruth

Babe Ruth was also known as "The Bambino" and the "Sultan of Swat."

Player Profile

BORN George Herman Ruth, Jr. was born on February 6, 1895, in Baltimore, Maryland.

FAMILY He was born to German-American parents George Herman Ruth, Sr. and Kate Schamberger-Ruth. He had a sister named Mamie. Ruth married Helen Woodford in 1914 and adopted one daughter, Dorothy Ruth, in 1921. He remarried in 1929 to Claire Merritt Hodgson.

EDUCATION Ruth attended St. Mary's Industrial School for Boys.

AWARDS Seven World Series championships, 1923 American League **Most Valuable Player (MVP),** two all-star selections, named to Major League Baseball (MLB) **All-Century Team,** inducted to the Baseball Hall of Fame in 1936

BABE RUTH
Pitcher/Outfielder

Early Years

Babe Ruth was born in a rough neighborhood of Baltimore. He left his parents at age seven and spent the next 12 years at St. Mary's Industrial School for Boys. There, he learned how to play baseball. Ruth was eventually spotted by Baltimore Orioles owner Jack Dunn. The Orioles were a **minor league** team at the time. They signed the 19-year-old as a pitcher. Ruth's new teammates called him "Jack's newest babe." The nickname "Babe" stuck.

In 1914, Ruth was sold to the Boston Red Sox. He pitched his first major league game on July 11 and led his team to a win. He won his first World Series with the Red Sox in 1915. Ruth played a larger role in the Red Sox 1916 World Series win, pitching a 14-inning **complete game** win in game 2. Although his pitching was impressive, Red Sox management wanted him hitting more. They placed Ruth in right field so he could play, and hit, in every game. In 1919, he set a record for most home runs in one season with 29.

Developing Skills

Ruth knew he was a good player and demanded higher pay. The Red Sox owner could not afford to keep him, and on December 26, 1919, Ruth was sold to the New York Yankees. In his first year with the Yankees, Ruth hit 54 home runs. His .847 **slugging percentage** was a major league record that stood until 2001. In 1921, Ruth hit 59 home runs and helped the Yankees earn their first American League championship.

By the time he retired in 1935, Ruth held 56 major league records. Many of these records stood for years before being topped. Some of his records stand today, including total bases (457), single season extra base hits (119), and times on base in one season (379).

Babe Ruth

Greatest Moment

Ruth is widely considered the greatest baseball player of all time. In 1927, he had one of his greatest seasons. He had spent years trying to beat his home run record of 59. Finally, on the second-to-last day of the season, Ruth hit his 60th home run.

Another one of Ruth's greatest moments came in the 1926 World Series. A young Yankees fan named Johnny Sylvester was in the hospital with an injury. Ruth heard of the boy's condition and promised Johnny he would hit a home run for him. Ruth came through on his promise, hitting three home runs in Game 4 of the World Series.

In 1923, the Yankees moved to Yankee Stadium, which is often called "The House That Ruth Built." That year, Ruth helped the Yankees win their first of many World Series.

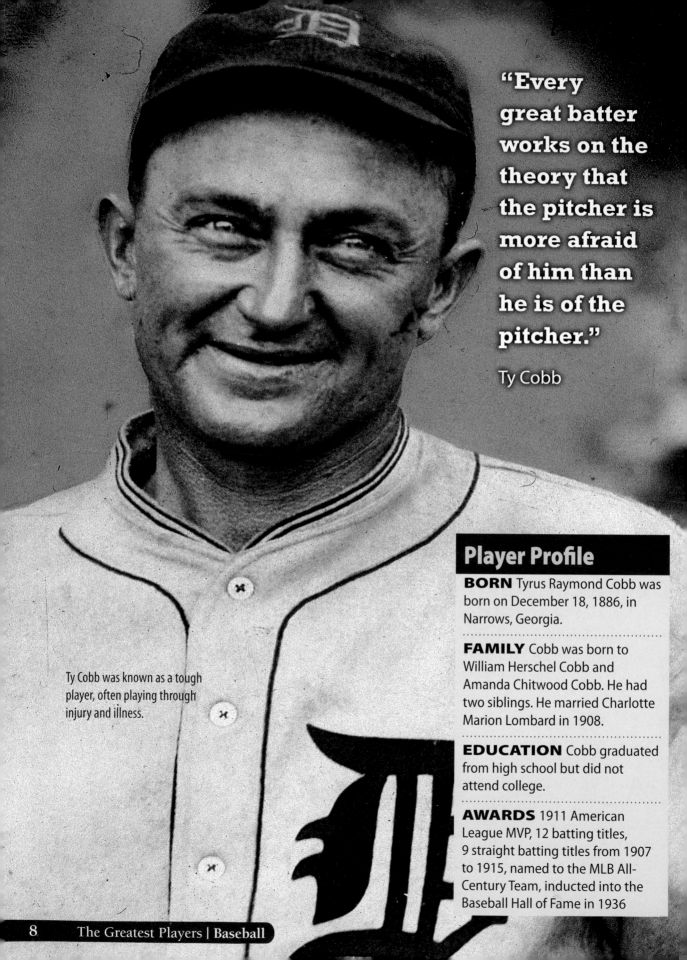

"Every great batter works on the theory that the pitcher is more afraid of him than he is of the pitcher."

Ty Cobb

Ty Cobb was known as a tough player, often playing through injury and illness.

Player Profile

BORN Tyrus Raymond Cobb was born on December 18, 1886, in Narrows, Georgia.

FAMILY Cobb was born to William Herschel Cobb and Amanda Chitwood Cobb. He had two siblings. He married Charlotte Marion Lombard in 1908.

EDUCATION Cobb graduated from high school but did not attend college.

AWARDS 1911 American League MVP, 12 batting titles, 9 straight batting titles from 1907 to 1915, named to the MLB All-Century Team, inducted into the Baseball Hall of Fame in 1936

TY COBB
Outfielder

Early Years

At age 14, Ty Cobb began playing semi-professional baseball with the Royston Rompers. In 1904, he joined the minor league Anniston Steelers. Cobb then began playing with the Augusta Tourists, where he continued to develop as a powerful baseball player. On August 20, 1905, the Tourists sold Cobb to the American League's Detroit Tigers. He played most of his professional career with the Tigers.

Developing Skills

In 1905, Cobb was the youngest player in the American League. He was 18 years old. Cobb was often hassled by older players, but he soon earned their respect through his hard work and impressive baseball skills. In 1906, Cobb became a starting center fielder, but it was at bat where he began to shine. That year, he had a **batting average** of .316 in 98 games. He went on to post a better than .316 batting average in every season for the rest of his career.

Throughout his career, Cobb was respected, and sometimes feared, as a tough opponent and a great baseball player. He held 90 Major League Baseball records, including highest career batting average (.366) and most career batting titles (12). Both of these records still stand today. His 4,189 career hits stood as a major league record until 1985, and his 2,245 career runs was the top mark until 2001. Cobb also held the record for most career stolen bases, with 892, until 1977.

Ty Cobb

Greatest Moment

In 1936, Cobb received 222 of a possible 226 votes during the first ever Baseball Hall of Fame vote. No other player has received this many votes to enter the Hall of Fame.

Though Cobb's career was full of great moments, his best season came in 1909. That year, he led the Tigers to their third straight American League **pennant**. Cobb also won his third straight batting title that season, with a batting average of .377. He recorded 107 **runs batted in (RBI)** and nine home runs. This earned him the **triple crown** award.

In 1909, Ty Cobb led the league with nine home runs. All nine home runs were "in the park," making him the only player to lead the league in home runs without hitting the ball out of the park.

9

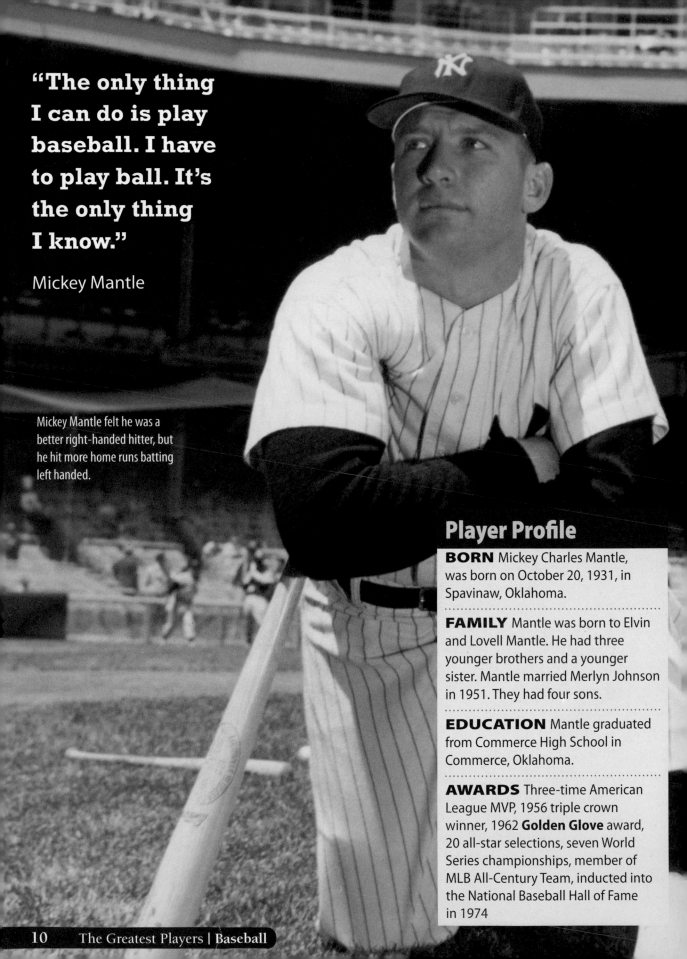

"The only thing I can do is play baseball. I have to play ball. It's the only thing I know."

Mickey Mantle

Mickey Mantle felt he was a better right-handed hitter, but he hit more home runs batting left handed.

Player Profile

BORN Mickey Charles Mantle, was born on October 20, 1931, in Spavinaw, Oklahoma.

FAMILY Mantle was born to Elvin and Lovell Mantle. He had three younger brothers and a younger sister. Mantle married Merlyn Johnson in 1951. They had four sons.

EDUCATION Mantle graduated from Commerce High School in Commerce, Oklahoma.

AWARDS Three-time American League MVP, 1956 triple crown winner, 1962 **Golden Glove** award, 20 all-star selections, seven World Series championships, member of MLB All-Century Team, inducted into the National Baseball Hall of Fame in 1974

Mickey Mantle
Outfielder

Early Years

As a child, Mickey Mantle played football, basketball, and baseball. Football nearly cost Mantle his life. During a high school football practice, he was kicked in the shin. The wound became infected. Mantle was treated and soon recovered. However, as a result of the infection, he had to live with a bone disease for the rest of his life.

In 1947, Mantle joined the Baxter Springs Whiz Kids of Kansas. The next year, a New York Yankees scout saw Mantle play and noted his great skill at **switch hitting**. The Yankees offered Mantle a contract to play with their minor league team in Independence, Kansas. Then, on April 17, 1951, Mantle played his first game with the Yankees. He played his entire major league career with the Yankees.

Developing Skills

In 1951, Mantle helped the Yankees win their 14th World Series championship. In the next season, Mantle moved from right field to center field, replacing Joe DiMaggio. This began a string of records and accomplishments for Mantle. He holds the World Series records for home runs (18), runs scored (42), and RBIs (40).

Mantle was known for his great hitting power. On September 10, 1960, he hit a ball 643 feet (196 meters) out of Brigg's Stadium in Detroit. In 1963, Mantle almost became the only player to hit a ball out of Yankee Stadium, when he hit a ball off the right field **facade**. In 18 years with the Yankees, Mantle appeared in 12 World Series. He is regarded by many as the greatest switch-hitter of all time.

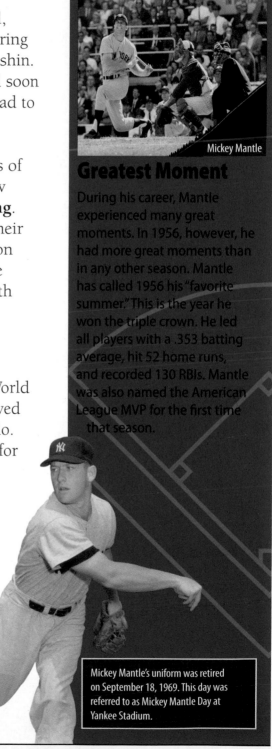

Mickey Mantle

Greatest Moment

During his career, Mantle experienced many great moments. In 1956, however, he had more great moments than in any other season. Mantle has called 1956 his "favorite summer." This is the year he won the triple crown. He led all players with a .353 batting average, hit 52 home runs, and recorded 130 RBIs. Mantle was also named the American League MVP for the first time that season.

Mickey Mantle's uniform was retired on September 18, 1969. This day was referred to as Mickey Mantle Day at Yankee Stadium.

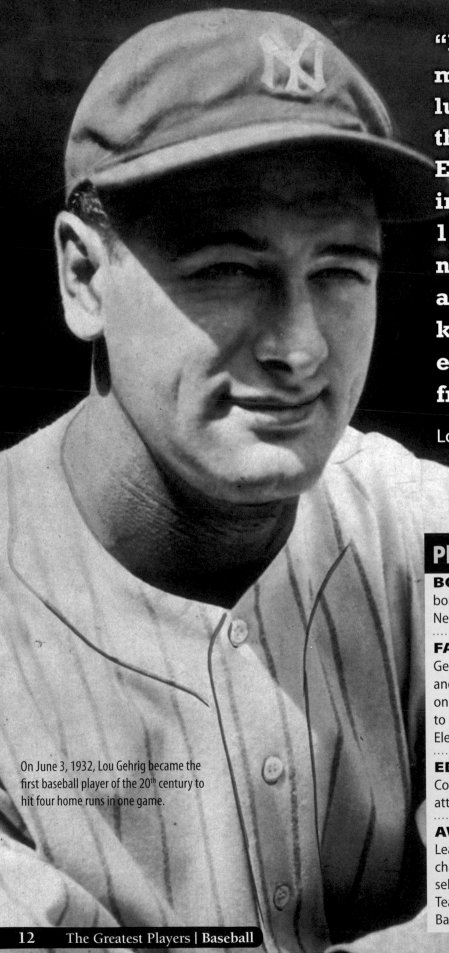

On June 3, 1932, Lou Gehrig became the first baseball player of the 20th century to hit four home runs in one game.

"I consider myself the luckiest man on the face of the Earth. I have been in ballparks for 17 years and have never received anything but kindness and encouragement from you fans."

Lou Gehrig

Player Profile

BORN Henry Louis Gehrig was born on June 19, 1903, in New York, New York.

FAMILY Gehrig was born to German-American parents Heinrich and Christina Gehrig. He was the only child of his parents' four children to live past infancy. Gehrig married Eleanor Twitchell in September 1933.

EDUCATION He graduated from Commerce High School and later attended Columbia University.

AWARDS Two-time American League MVP, six World Series championships, seven all-star selections, named to MLB All-Century Team, inducted into the National Baseball Hall of Fame in 1939

Lou Gehrig
First Baseman

Early Years

At age 17, Lou Gehrig was playing in a high school baseball game in what is now Wrigley Field in Chicago. In the ninth inning, Gehrig hit a **grand-slam** home run in front of a crowd of 6,000 people. No 17-year-old had ever hit the ball out of a major league park before. In 1923, Gehrig joined the Columbia University Lions as a pitcher and first baseman. He then caught the eye of a New York Yankees scout. Within two months, Gehrig had a contract with the Yankees. He began his 17-year career as a **pinch hitter** and first baseman. Gehrig saw little playing time over his first two years, but that soon changed.

Developing Skills

In 1926, Gehrig made a splash with a batting average of .313, hitting 47 doubles, 20 triples, 16 home runs, and 112 RBIs. The next year was even better, with Gehrig hitting .373, with 52 doubles, 18 triples, 47 home runs, and a record-setting 175 RBIs. The Yankees won the American League pennant and went on to **sweep** the Pittsburgh Pirates in the 1927 World Series.

Gehrig is known as one of the greatest batters of all time. From 1930 to 1932, he had 509 RBIs. Gehrig had 13 straight seasons where he hit 100 or more RBIs, seven seasons with 150 or more RBIs, eight seasons with 200 or more hits, and five seasons of 40 or more home runs. In 1931, Gehrig hit 184 RBIs, an American League record that still stands today. He also holds the record for most career grand slam home runs, with 23. His 2,130 consecutive games played stood as a record until Cal Ripken Jr. broke it in 1995.

Lou Gehrig

Greatest Moment

Perhaps the most amazing moment of Gehrig's career came on July 4, 1939, a day known as "Lou Gehrig Appreciation Day" in New York. Gehrig's game had been declining for months. In June 1939, he was diagnosed with a fatal disease that causes people to lose control of their muscles.

The Yankees held a retirement ceremony for Gehrig at Yankee Stadium. At end of the ceremony, Gehrig gave one of the most memorable speeches in the history of baseball.

Lou Gehrig's uniform was retired on July 4, 1939. He was the first player to receive such an honor in Major League Baseball history.

> "If there was ever a man born to be a hitter, it was me."
>
> Ted Williams

Ted Williams was often compared to New York Yankee Joe DiMaggio, his main rival. In fact, the two players were nearly traded for one another.

Player Profile

BORN Theodore Samuel Williams was born on August 30, 1918, in San Diego, California.

FAMILY Williams was born to Samuel Stuart Williams and May Venzor. He had one younger brother, Danny. Williams was married three times. He had three children, a son and two daughters.

EDUCATION Williams graduated from Herbert Hoover High School in San Diego, California.

AWARDS Two-time American League MVP, two triple crown titles, 19 all-star selections, named to MLB All-Century Team , inducted into the National Baseball Hall of Fame in 1966

Ted Williams
Outfielder

Early Years

Ted Williams grew up in the North Park neighborhood of San Diego. He first played baseball on the Herbert Hoover High School baseball team, where he became a star player. Soon, offers were coming his way from the St. Louis Cardinals and the New York Yankees. His mother, however, did not want Williams to leave school. She had him signed to the San Diego Padres, which was a minor league team at the time. From the beginning, Williams wanted to be known as "the greatest hitter who ever lived."

Developing Skills

In 1939, Williams was drafted to the major leagues, joining the Boston Red Sox as a left fielder. He led the American League in RBIs that year. Near the end of the 1941 season, Williams had a batting average of .400. No one had recorded a batting average that high for 11 years. His manager offered to give Williams the last two games off so he could keep the record. Williams, however, insisted on playing. "If I can't hit .400 all the way," he explained, "I don't deserve it." He went on to play a double-header and ended the season with an incredible .406 batting average.

No player has had a .400 batting average in a season since Williams. He was one of the greatest left-handed batters in baseball history. Throughout his 19-season career with the Red Sox, Williams set many impressive records. In 1949, he reached base in 84 consecutive games, a record that stands today. He set another record in 1957 when he reached a base in 16 consecutive at bat appearances. Williams had a career batting average of .344 and hit 521 home runs.

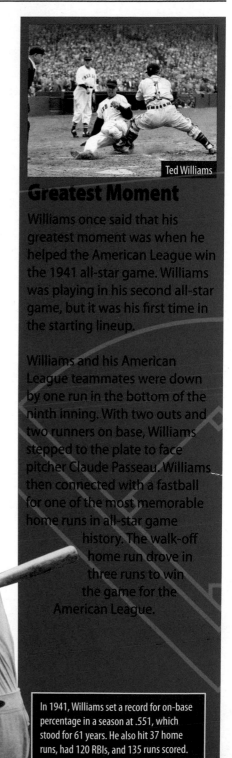

Ted Williams

Greatest Moment

Williams once said that his greatest moment was when he helped the American League win the 1941 all-star game. Williams was playing in his second all-star game, but it was his first time in the starting lineup.

Williams and his American League teammates were down by one run in the bottom of the ninth inning. With two outs and two runners on base, Williams stepped to the plate to face pitcher Claude Passeau. Williams then connected with a fastball for one of the most memorable home runs in all-star game history. The walk-off home run drove in three runs to win the game for the American League.

In 1941, Williams set a record for on-base percentage in a season at .551, which stood for 61 years. He also hit 37 home runs, had 120 RBIs, and 135 runs scored.

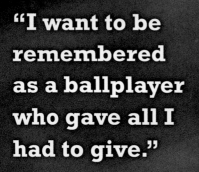

> **"I want to be remembered as a ballplayer who gave all I had to give."**
>
> Roberto Clemente

Roberto Clemente shares the record for most Golden Glove awards with another baseball great, Willie Mays.

Player Profile

BORN Roberto Clemente Walker was born on August 18, 1934, in Carolina, Puerto Rico.

FAMILY He was the youngest of seven children born to Don Melchor Clemente and Luisa Walker. Clemente married Vera Zabala. They had three sons, Roberto Jr., Luis Roberto, and Enrique Roberto.

EDUCATION Clemente graduated from Julio C. Vizarrondo High School in Carolina.

AWARDS 1966 National League MVP, 1971 World Series MVP, 1971 Babe Ruth Award for excellence in the World Series, 12 Golden Glove awards, two World Series championships, 15 all-star selections, inducted into the National Baseball Hall of Fame in 1973

Roberto Clemente
Outfielder

Early Years

As a child, Roberto Clemente played baseball with the neighborhood kids. Later, he started playing in amateur baseball leagues. He was soon offered a professional contract to play for the Santurce Crabbers in the Puerto Rican professional league. In his second season with the Crabbers, Clemente was the team's leading hitter. The Brooklyn Dodgers then offered him a contract to play on their minor league team, the Montreal Royals. It was not long before Pittsburgh Pirates scouts noticed Clemente's potential. In 1954, the Pirates **drafted** Clemente. He played his entire 18-year career with the Pirates.

Developing Skills

The Pittsburgh Pirates struggled in the 1950s, but Clemente was finding his game, both at the plate and in the field. During this time, Clemente spent several months serving in the United States Marine Corps Reserve. He credits his marine training with improving his athletic abilities. In 1960, things began to turn around for the Pirates. They won the National League and defeated the New York Yankees in seven games to win the World Series. Clemente ended the season with a .314 batting average and 16 home runs. He also established himself as a dominant outfielder. After 1960, Clemente batted over .300 every season except 1968, when his average was .291. He won his second World Series with the Pittsburgh Pirates in 1971, with a series-leading .414 batting average.

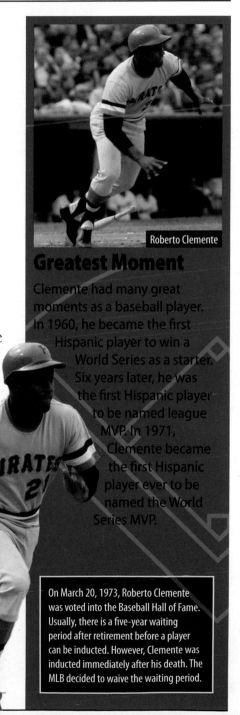

Roberto Clemente

Greatest Moment

Clemente had many great moments as a baseball player. In 1960, he became the first Hispanic player to win a World Series as a starter. Six years later, he was the first Hispanic player to be named league MVP. In 1971, Clemente became the first Hispanic player ever to be named the World Series MVP.

On March 20, 1973, Roberto Clemente was voted into the Baseball Hall of Fame. Usually, there is a five-year waiting period after retirement before a player can be inducted. However, Clemente was inducted immediately after his death. The MLB decided to waive the waiting period.

In 1950, Jackie Robinson starred in a movie about his life called *The Jackie Robinson Story*.

"I'm not concerned with your liking or disliking me...all I ask is that you respect me as a human being."

Jackie Robinson

Player Profile

BORN Jack Roosevelt Robinson was born on January 31, 1919, in Cairo, Connecticut.

FAMILY Robinson was born to Jerry and Mallie Robinson. He had three older brothers and an older sister. Robinson married Rachel Isum in 1946. They had two sons and one daughter.

EDUCATION He graduated from Pasadena Junior College and later attended the University of California in Los Angeles.

AWARDS 1945 Negro League all-star selection, 1947 Rookie of the Year, 1949 National League MVP, 1955 World Series champion, six all-star selections, member of MLB All-Century Team, inducted into the National Baseball Hall of Fame in 1962

Jackie Robinson
Second Baseman

Early Years

Jackie Robinson became involved in sports while in high school. He excelled in football, basketball, track and field, and baseball. In 1938, Robinson was elected to the All-Southland Junior College Team for baseball, where he was named MVP. He later joined the Kansas City Monarchs of the Negro American League as a shortstop, but he had his sights set on the major leagues.

Though there had been African Americans in the MLB in the late 1800s, no African American had played in the modern era. When the Brooklyn Dodgers drafted Robinson, he jumped at the chance to prove himself. Robinson joined the Dodgers' minor league team, the Montreal Royals, in 1945.

Developing Skills

In 1946, Robinson led the minor league with a .349 batting average. Switching from shortstop to second base, he had a .985 **fielding average** and was named MVP that year. On April 15, 1947, Robinson became the first African American to play major league baseball in the modern era. Robinson finished the season with 12 home runs, a .297 batting average, and a league-leading 29 stolen bases. He went on to win the first Rookie of the Year award ever given in baseball.

In 1949, Robinson earned the National League MVP award. That year, he tallied 37 stolen bases, 124 RBIs, and 122 runs scored. Though Robinson recorded his worst season as a baseball player in 1955, it was also the year the Brooklyn Dodgers won the World Series. They defeated the New York Yankees in seven games to claim their first championship.

Jackie Robinson

Greatest Moment

Robinson's greatest moment may have been on April 15, 1947. On that day, Robinson walked onto Ebbets Field in New York City. There were 26,623 fans in attendance to witness Robinson make history as a member of the Brooklyn Dodgers. Robinson did not waste any time in proving his right to be there. He scored the game-winning run to help the Dodgers win the game 5–3.

Jackie Robinson's number 42 uniform was retired on April 15, 1997, throughout the entire major league. This means no major league player can wear number 42.

> "My motto was always to keep swinging. Whether I was in a slump or feeling badly or having trouble off the field, the only thing to do was keep swinging."

Hank Aaron

Hank Aaron is second only to Barry Bonds in career home runs, with 755.

Player Profile

BORN Henry Louis Aaron was born on February 5, 1934, in Mobile, Alabama.

FAMILY Aaron was born to Herbert and Estella Aaron. He had seven siblings. He married Barbara Lucas in 1953. They had four children. In 1973, he was remarried to Billye Williams. They had one daughter.

EDUCATION Aaron attended Central High School and the Josephine Allen Institute.

AWARDS 1981 1957 National League MVP, 1957 World Series champion, 1970 Lou Gehrig Memorial Award winner, three Golden Glove awards, 24 all-star selections, member of MLB All-Century Team, inducted into the National Baseball Hall of Fame in 1982

Hank Aaron
Outfielder

Early Years

Growing up in Alabama, Hank Aaron played baseball with sticks and bottle caps. Neither high school he attended had a baseball team, so Aaron joined the semi-professional Mobile Black Bears instead. He soon earned a reputation as a powerful hitter. It was not long before MLB teams gave him a tryout.

After graduating high school, Aaron joined the Indianapolis Clowns of the Negro American League in 1952. Not long after, two major league teams offered Aaron a contract—the New York Giants and the Boston Braves. Aaron signed with the Braves and played with the Braves farm teams, the Eau Claire Bears and the Jacksonville Tars in the minor league. In 1953, he led the league in runs, 115, hits, 208, RBIs, 125, and a batting average of .362. Aaron was named league MVP.

Developing Skills

On March 13, 1954, the Milwaukee Braves called Aaron up to the major league. He hit a home run in that game and the team gave him a contract. In 1955, he won his first National League batting title, batting .314, with 27 home runs and 106 RBIs. *The Sporting News* named him "player of the year." From 1955 to 1973, Aaron hit 24 or more home runs each season. He is the only baseball player to hit 30 or more runs in a season at least 15 times. Aaron's ranks in the top five all-time in eight different batting categories, including hits, RBIs, and runs. He recorded 6,858 total bases, 2,297 RBIs, 1,477 extra-base hits, and 17 consecutive seasons with 150 or more base hits.

Hank Aaron

Greatest Moment

One of the greatest years of Aaron's career was 1957. That season, he had a batting average of .322. He also led the league with 44 home runs and 132 RBIs. Aaron hit a spectacular **walk-off home run** in front of the home crowd in Milwaukee and was carried off the field by his teammates. The home run clinched the pennant win for the Braves. Aaron was later named National League MVP. In the World Series, he batted .393, with three home runs and seven RBIs. The Braves beat the New York Yankees to win the World Series.

A great moment for Hank Aaron came on April 8, 1974, when he hit home run number 715, breaking the home run record held by baseball legend Babe Ruth.

> **"A pitcher's got to be good and he's got to be lucky to get a no hit game."**
>
> Cy Young

Cy Young's main catcher in Cleveland was Chief Zimmer. Zimmer often put a piece of beefsteak in his glove to absorb the hard pitches thrown by Young.

Player Profile

BORN Denton True "Cy" Young was born on March 29, 1867, in Gilmore, Ohio.

FAMILY Young was born to McKinzie Young, Jr. and Nancy Miller. He was the eldest of five children. Young married Robba Miller in 1892.

EDUCATION He completed sixth grade.

AWARDS 1903 World Series champion, pitched the first **perfect game** in MLB history, member of the MLB All-Century Team, inducted into the National Baseball Hall of Fame in 1937

Cy Young
Pitcher

Early Years

Cy Young grew up in a small farming community. He had to leave school after the sixth grade to help his father on the farm. Young liked to unwind from his farm work by playing baseball. As a young man, he played for a number of amateur baseball teams. Young alternated between pitching and second base. In 1889, he was invited to play for a minor league team in Canton, Ohio.

In 1890, Young's pitching caught the attention of the Cleveland Spiders. Young pitched his first major league game for the Spiders on August 6 and recorded an 8–1 win. In 1892, Young led the league in wins, 36, **earned run average (ERA)**, 1.93, and **shutouts**, 9. The next year, the league moved the pitcher's mound back five feet (1.5 m) to make it easier for batters to hit the ball. Most pitchers could not adjust to the change, but Young continued to perform.

Developing Skills

In 1901, Young was traded to the Boston Americans. He won the American League triple crown for pitchers that year by leading the league in wins, **strikeouts**, and ERA. In 1903, Young led the Boston Americans to victory over the Pittsburgh Pirates in the first ever World Series championship. He even helped out at the plate, driving in three runs in Game 5.

Young led the league in wins five times, in strikeouts twice, and in shutouts seven times. Young still holds MLB records for most career wins (511), innings pitched (7,355), games started (815), and complete games (749).

Cy Young

Greatest Moment

One of Young's greatest moments came on May 5, 1904. Philadelphia Athletics pitcher Rube Waddell had just pitched a game against Young's Boston Americans in which he gave up only one hit. He bragged to the media about how he would do it again, taunting Young to face him. Young responded coolly by pitching a perfect game. In fact, Waddell was the last batter up at the end of the game. He hit a **pop fly** and was caught out. Young called to him with a smile, "How do you like that, you hayseed?" It was the first perfect game pitched in American League history.

One year after Cy Young's death in 1955, the Cy Young Award was created to honor the best pitcher in baseball each year.

> ## "Maybe I was born to play ball. Maybe I truly was."
>
> Willie Mays

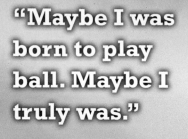

Willie Mays hit four home runs in one game on April 30, 1961, a feat accomplished by just 15 other players.

Player Profile

BORN William Howard Mays, Jr. was born on May 6, 1931, in Westfield, Alabama.

FAMILY Mays was born to William Mays, Sr. and Annie Satterwhite. He was raised by his Aunts Sarah and Ernestine. Mays married Margherite Wendell Chapman in 1956. They adopted one son, Michael.

EDUCATION Mays graduated from Fairfield Industrial High School.

AWARDS Two National League MVPs, 12 Golden Glove awards, 1951 Rookie of the Year, 1954 World Series champion, 24 all-star selections, member of MLB All-Century Team, inducted into the National Baseball Hall of Fame in 1979

Willie Mays
Outfielder

Early Years

Willie Mays grew up watching his father play baseball. His mother was a track and field athlete and basketball player. Mays followed in his mother's footsteps and excelled in basketball as well as football during high school. At age 16, Mays played for a professional baseball team while still in high school. A few months later, he went to Birmingham to play for the Black Barons in the Negro American League. Soon, MLB scouts took an interest in Mays. He signed to play for the New York Giants' affiliate in Trenton, New Jersey. He worked his way up to the Minneapolis Millers in 1951 and finished the season with an amazing .477 batting average. His skill with the bat and his excellent play in center field won him a spot in the majors.

Developing Skills

Mays played his first MLB season with the Giants in 1951. The Giants were underdogs when they met the Brooklyn Dodgers in the National League pennant final that year. Mays was next in line to bat when his teammate Bobby Thompson hit the "shot heard 'round the world" home run to win the pennant. The Giants did not win the World Series that season, but Mays won Rookie of the Year. He went on to win a league high 12 straight Golden Glove awards. He has also hit 30 or more home runs 11 times, including two 50 home run seasons. Mays played in 24 all-star games, a record he shares with legends Stan Musial and Hank Aaron. He has a career batting average of .302, with 660 home runs, 3,283 hits, and 1,903 RBIs. Mays is widely considered the greatest all around baseball player in MLB history.

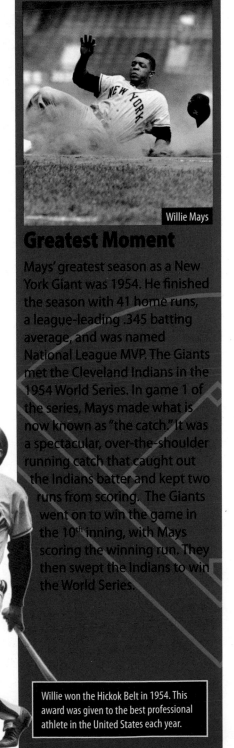

Willie Mays

Greatest Moment

Mays' greatest season as a New York Giant was 1954. He finished the season with 41 home runs, a league-leading .345 batting average, and was named National League MVP. The Giants met the Cleveland Indians in the 1954 World Series. In game 1 of the series, Mays made what is now known as "the catch." It was a spectacular, over-the-shoulder running catch that caught out the Indians batter and kept two runs from scoring. The Giants went on to win the game in the 10th inning, with Mays scoring the winning run. They then swept the Indians to win the World Series.

Willie won the Hickok Belt in 1954. This award was given to the best professional athlete in the United States each year.

Greatest Moments

1966
Roberto Clemente becomes the first Hispanic player to be named league MVP.

1926
Babe Ruth hits a home run for Johnny Sylvester.

1939
Lou Gehrig plays his 2,130th consecutive game.

1947
Jackie Robinson becomes the first African-American to play in the major league in the modern era.

1956
Mickey Mantle wins the Triple Crown.

1900	1910	1920	1930	1940	1950

1904
Cy Young pitches the first perfect game in the modern era of the MLB.

1928
Ty Cobb retires with the highest batting average of all time.

1941
Ted Williams hits the game-winning home run in the All-star game.

1951 – The Shot Heard 'Round the World

When: October 3, 1951

Where: New York, NY

The New York Giants were down 4–2 to the Brooklyn Dodgers when Bobby Thomson connected with what would come to be known as "the shot heard 'round the world." It was the bottom of the ninth inning in the deciding game of their pennant playoff series. With two runners on base, Thomson launched a homer into the left-field stands. The shot gave the Giants a 5–4 win.

1989 – K-Man

When: August 22, 1989

Where: Arlington, TX

Texas Rangers pitcher Nolan Ryan makes baseball history when he becomes the first pitcher to register 5,000 career strikeouts. Ryan was 42 years old and playing in his 21st major league season when he set the record. Ryan's 5,000th came off a 96-miles-per-hour fastball that beat hall-of-famer Rickey Henderson. Ryan retired in 1993 with 5,714 career strikeouts and a record of seven no-hitters.

1974
Hank Aaron breaks Babe Ruth's career home run record when he hits the 715th homer of his career.

1995 – Baseball's Iron Man

When: September 20, 1998

Where: Baltimore, MD

Cal Ripken, Jr. broke Lou Gehrig's iron man record for most consecutive games played. Gehrig's record, which many considered unbreakable, had stood for 56 years before Ripken surpassed it. Ripken's iron man streak would not come to an end for another 501 games. On September 20, Ripken voluntarily took himself out of the starting lineup to end his streak at 2,632 games. The streak spanned 17 seasons, all played with the Baltimore Orioles.

1960   1970   1980   1990   2000

1954
Willie Mays makes "the catch" in the World Series match-up against the Cleveland Indians.

2001 – Home Run King

When: October 5, 2001

Where: Los Angeles, CA

San Francisco Giant Barry Bonds slugged his 73rd home run of the season to set a new single-season home run record. The shot came in the last game of the season for the Giants and capped off the best season of Bonds' career. This season also saw Bonds set a new record for slugging percentage at .863, passing the former record of .847 set by Babe Ruth in 1920. Bonds would go on to play for another six seasons. Though he would never again reach the incredible batting numbers of his 2001 season, he did pass Hank Aaron as the all-time home run leader. Bonds finished his career with 762 home runs.

Write a Biography

Life Story

A person's life story can be the subject of a book. This kind of book is called a biography. Biographies often describe the lives of people who have achieved great success. These people may be alive today, or they may have lived many years ago. Reading a biography can help you learn more about a great person.

Get the Facts

Use this book, and research in the library and on the Internet, to find out more about your favorite baseball player. Learn as much about this player as you can. What team did this person play for? What are his or her statistics in important categories? Has this person set any records? Be sure to also write down key events in the person's life. What was this person's childhood like? What has he or she accomplished? Is there anything else that makes this person special or unusual?

Use the Concept Web

A concept web is a useful research tool. Read the questions in the concept web on the following page. Answer the questions in your notebook. Your answers will help you write a biography.

Roger Clemens was one of the most dominant pitchers of his era. He was the first pitcher to record 20 strikeouts in a single game, and he did it twice.

Concept Web

- What did you learn from the books you read in your research?
- Would you suggest these books to others?
- Was anything missing from these books?

- Where does this individual currently reside?
- Does he or she have a family?

- Where and when was this person born?
- Describe his or her parents, siblings, and friends.
- Did this person grow up in unusual circumstances?

Your Opinion

Adulthood

Childhood

WRITING A BIOGRAPHY

Main Accomplishments

Help and Obstacles

Work and Preparation

- What is this person's life's work?
- Has he or she received awards or recognition for accomplishments?
- How have this person's accomplishments served others?

- Did this individual have a positive attitude?
- Did he or she receive help from others?
- Did this person have a mentor?
- Did this person face any hardships?
- If so, how were the hardships overcome?

- What was this person's education?
- What was his or her work experience?
- How does this person work; what is the process he or she uses?

Know your STUFF!

1 Who is the current all-time leader in home runs?

2 What is the Triple Crown for batters?

3 Who was the first pitcher to throw a perfect game in the modern era of the MLB?

4 In what year did Babe Ruth hit what was then a record 60 home runs in a season?

5 What record did Ty Cobb set in 1928 that still stands today?

6 Who is regarded by many as the greatest switch hitter of all time?

7 On June 3, 1932, Lou Gehrig became the first player in the modern era to do what?

8 Who was the first Hispanic player to be named league MVP?

9 Who was the last player to finish a season with a batting average of .400 or better?

10 In 1947, Jackie Robinson became the first African American in the major league when he played with which team?

ANSWERS: 1. Barry Bonds 2. When one player finishes the season with the highest batting average, the most home runs, and the most RBIs 3. Cy Young 4. 1927 5. Highest career batting average of .366 6. Mickey Mantle 7. Hit four home runs in one game 8. Roberto Clemente 9. Ted Williams in 1941 with an average of .406 10. The Brooklyn Dodgers

Glossary

All-Century Team: a list of the 30 greatest players of the 20th century, as chosen by a vote from baseball fans

base: one of three areas spread around the infield that must be reached by runners in order to score a run

base hit: a hit that results in the batter reaching a base safely

batting average: the average number of base hits a player records per attempts at bat

complete game: when a pitcher plays an entire game from start to finish

drafted: chosen to play for a major league team

earned run average (ERA): the average number of runs a pitcher allows per nine innings pitched

facade: the front facing part of a building

fielding average: a measure of a defensive player's performance in handling a ball that has been hit or thrown toward them

golden glove: award given each year to players judged to be the best in their position

grand slam: a home run hit with runners on all three bases; scores four runs

home runs: a hit that results in the ball traveling over the outfield fence; scores the batter and any runners on base

innings: a period of play; there are nine innings in a major league game

minor league: a league below the major league; minor league teams are usually associated with major league teams in order to develop the skills of their players

Most Valuable Player (MVP): the player judged to be the most valuable to his team's success

pennants: league championships for both the National and American Leagues; the two pennant winners face off in the World Series

perfect game: when a pitcher completes a game without allowing any batters to get on base

pinch hitter: a hitter who takes the place of another player in the lineup

pop fly: a ball that flies high into the air after being hit by a batter

runs: when players safely cross home plate to score points for their team

runs batted in (RBI): a hit that results in a base runner scoring a run

shutout: when a pitcher completes a game without allowing any runs to be scored

slugging percentage: a statistic used to judge the power of a hitter; based on total bases earned divided by number of attempts at bat

strikeout: when a batter fails to hit the ball three times; results in the batter being ruled out

sweep: when a team defeats its opponent in a playoff series without losing a game

switch hitting: batters who can hit either left- or right-handed

triple crown: refers to batters who lead the league in batting average, runs batted in, and home runs

walk-off home run: a game-winning home run hit in the bottom of the last inning to immediately end the game

Index

Log on to www.av2books.com

AV² by Weigl brings you media enhanced books that support active learning. Go to www.av2books.com, and enter the special code found on page 2 of this book. You will gain access to enriched and enhanced content that supplements and complements this book. Content includes video, audio, web links, quizzes, a slide show, and activities.

Audio
Listen to sections of the book read aloud.

Video
Watch informative video clips.

Embedded Weblinks
Gain additional information for research.

Try This!
Complete activities and hands-on experiments.

WHAT'S ONLINE?

Try This!	Embedded Weblinks	Video	EXTRA FEATURES
Try a baseball activity.	Learn more about baseball players.	Watch a video about baseball.	
Test your knowledge of baseball equipment.	Read about baseball coaches.	View stars of the sport in action.	
Complete a mapping activity.	Find out more about where baseball games take place.	Watch a video about baseball players.	

 Audio
Listen to sections of the book read aloud.

 Key Words
Study vocabulary, and complete a matching word activity.

 Slide Show
View images and captions, and prepare a presentation.

 Quizzes
Test your knowledge.

AV² was built to bridge the gap between print and digital. We encourage you to tell us what you like and what you want to see in the future.
Sign up to be an AV² Ambassador at www.av2books.com/ambassador.